Ship Happens!

A Tiger Cruise Tale

How to
Spend Six Nights on a Navy Warship for $70

A Memoir by

Timothy J. Richards

Jim Richards

AuthorHouse™
1663 Liberty Drive, Suite 200
Bloomington, IN 47403
www.authorhouse.com
Phone: 1-800-839-8640

AuthorHouse™ UK Ltd.
500 Avebury Boulevard
Central Milton Keynes, MK9 2BE
www.authorhouse.co.uk
Phone: 08001974150

First published by AuthorHouse 8/9/2007

ISBN: 978-1-4259-9796-0 (sc)

TimothyJRichards@aol.com

Library of Congress Control Number: 2007901368

Printed in the United States of America
Bloomington, Indiana

This book is printed on acid-free paper.

Navy Department Library, Naval Historical Center, Washington Navy Yard, DC
Dudley Knox Library, Naval Postgraduate School, Monterey, CA
Naval War College Library, Historical Collection, Newport, RI

Bloomington, IN  Milton Keynes, UK

ACKNOWLEDGEMENTS

I'd like to thank my editor, Rob Kaplan of Cortlandt Manor, New York, for his helpful email assistance, friendly telephone support, and for guiding me through the process of crafting my memoir. His advice made this a better book.

Betz Richards

I'd also like to thank Betz Richards, my loving wife of twenty years, for her patience and support in critiquing my work; and to my daughter Corrin "Stomper" Stamatakos: thanks for sharing the adventure with me.

Corrin Barry Stamatakos

DEDICATION

This memoir is dedicated to all the men and women of the United States Armed Forces who have served or are presenting serving in *Operation Enduring Freedom* in Afghanistan and *Operation Iraqi Freedom* in Iraq. It is also dedicated to my son, EN1(SW)Timothy F. Richards, who answered the call of Freedom on September 11, 2001, and enlisted in the United States Navy.

CONTENTS

June 13, 1999

"TIMMY'S GONE," I said to my wife while I came through the side door entrance to the house and into the kitchen. She sat up from the recliner and looked around at me. When I announced, "His apartment's empty," her face drooped.

"What do you mean?" Betz asked. "Where is he?"

"I don't know. All of his furniture is gone, and there's a lot of trash lying around on the floor. And all that other stuff we bought him—it's gone."

"What?"

"Yeah, gone."

"What do you mean all that furniture we bought him is gone?"

"That's right," I said. "The place is empty and it's a mess."

Betz's eyebrows tensioned. "Where is he?" she said in total disbelief. "Where could he be?"

Just the day before, Timmy had sat with us in our dining room eating Betz's tender pork loin smothered in sweet red cabbage and apple rings. He was in high spirits opening presents and celebrating his eighteenth birthday. Laughing freely at the dinner table, he shared his fun with us and a couple of his buddies he had brought along to help celebrate his newly acquired freedom. Timmy was relaxed and confident, his conversation free. Betz and I knew how much he had looked forward to his emancipation, but now, twenty-four hours later, he was gone—vanished without a word.

"After all we did for that kid," I muttered.

A deadpan look settled over Betz's face. "I just don't get it," she said.

FOR SIX YEARS Timmy lived with us before returning to Florida in 1997 to reunite with his mother. She and I had agreed to a change in custody. He was to remain with her and not bounce back and forth between families. But he did anyway. On an August morning the following year, down on his money and luck, he boarded a Greyhound bus and headed north to Cleveland. He was seventeen years old. But now he was eighteen and gone.

NO LONGER CONSTRAINED, Timmy was wildly liberated—released from the binding chains of parental authority and his adolescent bond to childhood. He was free at last, launched under his own power to find his own way, unlike the way his parents or social authorities had prescribed. Now he could choose his own direction. His new compass heading: due south.

Delighted with his legal authority to purchase property, Timmy bought a $300 Buick and blew out of town on a set of radials as bald as a baby's butt. He cranked up the Buick[1], pointed it south, and headed for Cape Coral, but wound up three hours later in Pittsburgh before he realized he was heading east. It was his first road trip; he had left without a map. All that he took were a few personal items, his last Burger King paycheck, and a full tank of high-octane adventure that fueled his driving spirit to see his friends in Florida.

It wasn't long before I discovered his whereabouts when his mother called a few days later. While I sat back and listened to her tell the story of his arrival, I imagined Timmy on the interstate for the first time, tapping out the rhythm of country music and daydreaming of good old times in Cape Coral. I could see his heavy-laden eyelids drooping while his head nodded to the monotony of the road. I visualized him at a Georgia truck stop, deep asleep on the front seat, and waking up with a sweaty oily feeling on his face and a bad taste in his mouth. I thought of him arching his back and stretching, pushing in the cigarette lighter and pulling out a smoke, and thinking that a bacon double cheeseburger and a Coke sounded good.

Timmy settled down in Florida with his old friends and focused on earning a living. Over the next two years he worked six jobs, only to find that employers did not share his sense of ambition. With his goals hampered and his employment life going nowhere, he decided to make a change and interviewed with the largest employer in America: the United States Government. He was undecided about joining the service, but still visited the armed forces recruiting office in Fort Myers to get the scoop on military jobs. But during the time he spent in Florida searching for direction, I was afraid our personal relationship might drift apart. It didn't. It got closer, and a genuine friendship developed between us.

THEN THE WORLD CHANGED. One dreadful morning on September 11, 2001, a ruthless Islamic terrorist group, *al-Qa'ida,* attacked the United States of America, killing 2973 innocent civilians in

---

[1] Six years later Tim wrote: "Shortly after arriving in Florida, July 3 to be specific, I was changing the valve cover gasket on my 1985 Buick Regal since oil was leaking all over the engine. It was the first time I had done more than just minor work on a car, and I wound up dropping one of the cover bolts. I couldn't find it, and since I was doing the work in a field, I figured the bolt was lost in the grass. When I was done with the work, I drove to Circle K for a beverage. The engine froze up. A buddy came over with some jumper cables to give me the boost to break the engine free. Sure as shit, the engine broke free, literally. I blew a piston. As it turned out, the bolt had dropped into the valve cover area and wedged under a valve at 2000 rpm. I knew I was driving on borrowed time. My buddies and I went to Crystal Lake that night and beat the hell out of the Buick. Coming home from the lake the next day (July 4), less than 100 yards from the house, the motor finally blew. It looked like one of those NASCAR racecars when they blow their engines. Smoke billowed from the rear as we coasted to the end of the road, and that was the car's final destination."

the twin towers of the World Trade Center in New York City, the Pentagon in Washington, D.C., and on United Airlines flight 93 when it crashed near Shanksville in the rural farmlands of western Pennsylvania. Following the vicious sneak attack planned by the murdering *Osama bin Laden*, the rejected son of a Saudi Arabian billionaire, President George W. Bush relentlessly prosecuted al-Qa'ida in a global war against terrorism that began in Afghanistan and spilled over a year and a half later into Iraq against the repressive régime of Saddam Hussein. As the United States Government made war in Afghanistan, Tim's patriotism stirred his sense of duty. Four months after 9/11, my telephone rang.

"Dad, how ya doin'?"

"Yo, Tim. I'm doing fine. How are you?" It was good to hear his voice again. In a sudden flashback to my teenage years, I recalled my mother's voice when I often slept away from home as a guest of friends in the City of Euclid. When she would finally locate me at one of their houses on the weekend, Mom would plead, "Please call me more often and tell me where you are and what you're doing."

I was selfishly adrift from my family during my high school years, not caring about my mother or her feelings. But now, listening to Tim on the other end of the line, I knew what it meant to hear the voice of a child calling home.

In the past when Tim telephoned, he often had news of his recent accomplishments. I wondered what news he was bringing that day.

"Dad, do you remember that letter you sent me, the one where you said if I didn't do something with my life, I'd hover around that ten dollar an hour job for the rest of my life?"

I paused, but didn't answer.

"Well, I joined the United States Navy," he said.

I almost dropped the phone. "Tim's joined the Navy," I yelled to Betz, who was working a crossword puzzle in the family room.

"What? You're kidding!" she exclaimed, dropping her jaw as she got out of her seat.

Tim was finally doing something with his life.

TIM WAS SWORN IN for a six-year hitch on March 18, 2002, guaranteeing him a job with advanced technical training and automatic promotion to petty officer in twelve months. But *Operation Enduring Freedom* in Afghanistan was still hot. Although the *Taliban*, Afghanistan's ruling faction and cradle of Islamic fascism had been routed by December 2001, Osama bin Laden was still alive. He had escaped and was believed to be hiding in the mountains near Pakistan. The murdering bastard was still on the run.

On March 20, 2003, one year after Tim's enlistment, the war on terrorism continued as the United States launched *Operation Iraqi Freedom* against Saddam Hussein[2] and the nation of Iraq. Two weeks earlier on March 5, Tim had been deployed on an eight-month tour of the Persian Gulf, on the mighty warship USS Bridge (AOE 10), a fast combat supply ship in support of the USS Nimitz nuclear aircraft carrier. He was headed for war in the Middle East.

Three months later on June 21, Tim's wife Sharon gave birth to their first child—my first grandchild—Emily Samantha Richards[3]. It was an anxious time for them—Tim being in the Persian Gulf and Sharon being without him in the delivery room. Rapid-fire emails shot back and forth between Tim and me. I called the Red Cross several times, pleading Tim's case to be released from duty on emergency leave, but Tim could not come home. Thanks to modern technology, however, an attending nurse in the delivery room photographed the delivery and emailed the pictures of Emily's birth to Tim.

In August, after five months at sea, Tim emailed from the gulf, stating that the USS Bridge had been selected to conduct a Tiger Cruise, a public relations event sponsored by the Navy for the benefit of family members of sailors returning from the Iraq War. According to a Navy librarian, the program may have been established in the 1970s as *Operation Tiger*. It allowed sailors to bring their young children, called "tigers," for a short trip at sea. The definition of tiger evidently evolved to include adults; however, my original invitation to the cruise excluded spouses. Apparently, the Navy didn't want any hanky-panky at sea. But I was not a spouse, and I looked forward to the adventure with my own two tigers when Tim invited his sister Corrin on the cruise. I hoped she and I could join him in Pearl Harbor, Oahu, for the last leg of his Naval deployment on a six-night Tiger Cruise from Hawaii to Bremerton Naval Base, Washington.

---

[2] Saddam Hussein, the deposed dictator of Iraq, was executed on December 30, 2006. Iraqis cheered after he was hanged for causing the deaths of 148 Shiite in 1982. Saddam Hussein struggled after American military guards handed him over to Iraqi executioners, but grew calm in his final moments while masked executioners slipped a black cloth and noose around his neck. Saddam refused the hood to cover his eyes. Iraqi television showed a video of his body wrapped in a shroud, the head uncovered, and the neck twisted at an angle. Witnesses to the execution cheered around the body of Saddam after the hanging—three years after he was hauled from a "spider" hole in the ground by U.S. military forces.

[3] Sharon wrote: "Although my husband was at sea, I was not alone when I delivered Emily. Tim's mother was with me. Signe had arrived from Florida on the 19th. I just got lucky that she came when she did. My anticipated delivery date was the 27th, but the baby came six days early on the 21st, which, by the way, is the antonym of Tim's and my birthday, the 12th. Emily was 6 pounds, 5.7 ounces, and 21.5 inches long. I think I must have been the luckiest lady in the world. I had top-notch medical care and a wonderful support system. I was as healthy as could be expected being pregnant, and I was married to a wonderful man serving in the military that would have been there with me if he could. Both my immediate and extended families gave the baby and me so much emotional support. Things may not have been ideal with Tim being gone, but I couldn't have asked for anything more than him being safe, my daughter being healthy, and the wonderful people in my life being there to help me through it all."

BUT THERE WAS A PROBLEM. Initially, I had decided not to take the cruise because of a trip to Italy I had already booked. There was also the problem of money: the cost of the trip to Hawaii added to the expense of Italy. The USS Bridge would dock in Bremerton, Washington, at 3:00 p.m., and thirty-six hours later I had to board an airplane in Cleveland for Italy. I was afraid I couldn't make the connection because of possible delays. It was too risky, and I wasn't sure about Corrin's work schedule either. She had just started a new job. If she elected to go, I wondered if her employer would understand. And what about her expense? She was saving to get married in six months.

Nevertheless, I needed someone to represent the Richards family onboard the BRIDGE, someone to accompany Tim when he greeted his wife and baby. The family reunion was too important to miss. So I called Corrin in Chicago and told her about my problem with the airline schedule and asked her if she had accepted her brother's invitation. Undecided at first, she hesitated when I asked, "Are you interested in taking the trip without me?" I had anticipated her not going and decided in advance to ante up half the expense as an incentive then doubled the amount in a second round of bidding. She graciously accepted. I was relieved and pleased. She would be the family ambassador, and I would get to send her on another exciting world trip, like the one Betz and I had sent her on in Europe when she studied at the Miami University campus in Luxembourg for one semester in her sophomore year.

However, I was still deeply disappointed. I had to stay home and miss the reunion. It saddened me to think I would miss my son greeting his family. But all was not lost. Betz's brain had shifted into overdrive.

MY WIFE WAS A PROBLEM SOLVER. The promise of my own Tiger Cruise had lingered in her mind. One morning, while working in the kitchen chopping carrots, Betz chimed in with a delightful solution.

"Take the trip anyway," she said, "even though the flight schedule is tight. I'll pay for the trip—both trips—yours and Corrin's."

My eyebrows dipped. Was she serious?

"You can do this," she said.

While I watched Betz slice the carrots into little rounds to sweeten the stew on the stove, she drew back her lips and curled them up at the corners. Her mischievous smile reminded me of a cat that had just swallowed a canary.

"Do you really think I can?" I asked.

"Sure, Tim. If anyone can, it's you."

"That's it!" I declared, pumping a clinched fist. "I'll go!"

* * * * *

Tuesday, October 28, 2003

BETZ WOKE ME at 5:15 a.m. She was already awake and reading one of her true crime books in bed. She only needed about five hours of sleep each night and occupied the remaining quiet hours by reading. As long as I have known my wife, she has been a light sleeper, so when it came to getting up early to catch a plane, I didn't need an alarm. I had Betz.

"Tim, it's time to get up," she said. "There's no sleeping in this morning."

Thirty minutes later we were downstairs for a bite of breakfast then out the door and rolling down the interstate. It was a quick trip to the airport: ten minutes. Although at that early hour the roads were empty, the curbside drop off at Cleveland Hopkins International was already busy with travelers waiting to check their baggage.

I leaned across the center console to kiss Betz goodbye and thought about her being alone for the next ten days. She had to cover the operation of my business, but I knew she could handle it. She had been a former partner in our insurance agency for fifteen years; she still had her license. Betz leaned over and returned my affection, while I held her hand in my palm. It was warm. I knew I would miss her.

"I love you sweetheart," I said. "I'll see you when I get back."

"I love you too," she said. "Have a safe trip, and be sure to hug little Emily for me—and Timmy and Sharon—Corrin too!"

"I will."

"Oh, have you got your ticket?"

"Yes."

"Are you sure?"

"Yes, dear. I'm sure."

"Okay. I've got your itinerary, so when you get back . . . uh . . . Oh, never mind. I'll take care of it. Good-bye."

"Good-bye honey. See you soon."

I stepped into line to check my bag. It wasn't long before the familiar smell of cigarette smoke drifted by. I could always depend on someone smoking outside the terminal door. Curbside was the last place to light one up.

"How many bags, sir?" queried the Sky Cap, while he reached for my reservation.

"Just one, plus a carry-on."

He confirmed my reservation, checked my bag, and nodded politely when I tipped him. Tilting his head toward the lobby door, he spoke in a courteous tone.

"You're all set, sir. Have a good flight."

I still needed a boarding pass, so I headed for the electronic check-in. Since the days of handwritten tickets in 1962 when I first flew on an airplane while serving in the U.S. Army, ticketing had changed. Today, reservations and boarding passes download online and confirmations dispense from a machine at the terminal. Swipe your card and check your bag. That's all it takes to get onboard.

I HEADED FOR THE SECURITY GATE. Since the attack on 9/11 and the devastation brought on by four highjacked airliners, airport security was strict. I didn't mind the scrutiny, but when the dreaded alarm went off as I passed through the gate, my opinion quickly changed.

"Great," I mumbled when a uniformed guard waved at me.

"Would you please step over here," he asked, pointing to an isolated area where my life was about to become public.

It was my turn in the fishbowl, I thought, a little public humiliation in the name of national security. It seemed that everyone was looking at me when he signaled with a security wand to a spot on the floor where I was to stand.

"Please turn around, spread your legs, and raise your arms."

Dutifully, I obeyed. The flush of embarrassment reddened my face as he waved the hand-held metal detector over and around and up and down my limbs. Interesting thoughts conjured up in my mind: images of women gawking. While they eyeballed my body and spread-eagled legs, I wondered what they saw. When the sideshow ended, I gathered my personal items from the conveyor tray and grabbed my carry-on bag.

Luggage-toting passengers milled around the concourse buying last minute items and drinking coffee. I had an hour to wait, so I followed my nose to the Starbucks stand, bought a cup, and lingered around the storefronts sipping dark roast and dodging oncoming travelers. In the distance I noticed a two-man shoeshine stand. While one man brushed up a shine on the shoes of a customer perched on a yellow vinyl chair, the other man invited passing pedestrians to take a seat.

"Good morning," I said when I approached. "How you fellas doin' today?"

"Just fine," the taller one answered.

"Have you got a few minutes for a shine?" I asked, indicating with my hand that I was ready to mount the second chair.

"Yes, sir," he chirped. "Have a seat."

His name was China, a tall pleasant fellow attentive to his work. His inquisitive nature queried about my destination, and when I told him I was on my way to Pearl Harbor as a guest of the United States Navy, he said,

"That's cool." China smiled curiously at me while he whipped up a bright rag shine on my Florsheim shoes. Thankful when he realized my son was coming home after eight months of duty in the Iraq War, he said, "That's a blessing," then nodded his head with approval.

When I began to preach a long list of benefits associated with joining the service, his attention peaked. China paused, stood straight up, then leaned back and shifted his weight to one foot. In a playful tone he announced,

"I've already interviewed with a Navy recruiter. I'm signing up in June."

"That's cool," I quipped.

I BOARDED THE PLANE and thought about the expense of the trip. Thanks to a special Web site Tim had suggested, the official Tiger Cruise travel agency that assisted hundreds of families with airline tickets and hotel arrangements, two round trip tickets for Corrin and me, including one night in Waikiki, cost $1400. That plus $70 in cash, payable onboard to the Navy for food, rounded out my initial expense.

The plane lifted off the tarmac and sliced through the gray blanket hovering over Cleveland. An hour later the plane was cruising over the Great Plains of America and the vast beauty of the Midwest. I looked down at the countless patches of green farmland neatly squared off, a natural checkerboard connected by an intricate web of rivers and roads. The gray shadows cast from the clouds created a Dalmatian-like effect on the earth, scattering across the landscape and spotting the ground below. And the farther west I flew, the browner the landscape became. Dotting the arid land, however, was evidence of irrigation in the shape of green circles with long watering pipes mounted on wheels that rotated like giant hands on a great water clock.

Soon afterwards, desert foothills replaced the fields of winter wheat, foothills embedded with empty canyons connected by red ravines. There were dry riverbeds and sliver thin roadways. Overlaying the beautiful vista was a fleecy layer of cumulus puffs of rippled clouds that reminded me of my childlike vision of heaven.

The droning of the turbine engines lulled me into peace, and in that captivated state I recalled a 1963 black and white television show hosted by Rod Serling: *The Twilight Zone*. One of the frightening, but memorable teleplays, *Nightmare at 20,000 Feet*, took place outside an airliner during flight. While a passenger (*actor* William Shatner) stared out the portal, he spotted a gremlin on the tip of the wing. It inched its way towards the window, struggling to keep its balance against a powerful wind. When it finally reached the fuselage, the creature attached itself to the passenger's window and glared menacingly at the horrified man. I glanced outside my portal and checked the tip of the wing.

I awoke from a short nap to the vast wastelands of Colorado—shades of gray, browns, and tans inner-mixed with vermilion and drab greens. Flat mesas stood as sentries. Deep canyons cut the barren landscape. Dry riverbeds meandered—nature's handiwork indeed. Lengthy lines of mountain spines reached for the horizon and gave way to dry desert beds that flattened into great desolate seas of sand. Isolated railroad tracks and empty roads dissected the landscape, roads as straight as a draftsman's ruler, lonely roads that seemed to go nowhere.

THE USUAL LAYER of hazy smog smothered the Los Angeles basin when the plane landed. The flight arrived forty-five minutes before my next flight departed. Quickly, I mapped out a route to Hawaiian Air through an intricate maze of interconnecting corridors and conveyor belts, a fifteen-minute workout lugging my bag behind me.

I approached the Hawaiian Air waiting area and reminisced about how fast Corrin had grown up. I flashed back to her childhood and recalled how cute she looked standing in front of the television in her Wonder Woman pajamas. She was a spirited four-year old and showed signs of becoming a cheerleader even then when she threw her arms up as a referee and yelled touchdown every time the Cleveland Browns scored.

While attending an Ohio high school cheer-off camp at Kent State University for varsity squads, Corrin was one of only nineteen cheerleaders from ten schools to be chosen as an All American Cheerleader. She worked two jobs that summer and saved $1100, the amount she needed to meet her expense. On January 1, 1996, she performed, along with her peers, in the half-time show at the Florida Citrus Bowl in Orlando, Florida. For a few exciting moments the ABC television network focused on her performance, her fleeting claim to fame.

Now, it was not that long ago that she was still in college and surprising us at home with unexpected weekend visits.

"Hi Dad, I'm home," she'd call out to us while rushing through the front door. Corrin would blow into town like a welcome wind, dragging her laundry bag and three pieces of luggage with her. It has always puzzled me why college kids need so much baggage for a weekend visit. By Sunday she'd be gone.

Before she graduated from Miami University, Corrin had been offered a job by AT&T as a sales representative. After graduating in June 2000, she signed on with them and moved to Georgia for training. Adapting quickly and being well liked by her peers, Corrin was invited to stay in Atlanta and train new employees, but after a year of southern sun and shady corporate politics, she became discouraged and interviewed *again* with AT&T, this time with their sales division in Chicago. She was twenty-three years old. Corrin moved to the Windy City, where she met her husband-to-be, Timothy Louis Stamatakos, an AT&T sales manager in commercial accounts. There would soon be three Tims in the family.

CORRIN SPOTTED ME weaving through the crowd. Excited, she jumped up and greeted me with a hug. I asked about her new job with Kendall Healthcare. By that time she had already quit AT&T for a more lucrative position in the health care industry. Following intensive training in specialized medical equipment used in connection with intensive care units and cardiac catheterization labs, Corrin was hired as a medical equipment sales representative in the Chicago area.

Within a few minutes we were standing in line with our boarding passes. Corrin had a carry-on bag and a book. She had always loved to read and brought along a motivational think-about-life kind of story: *The Five People You Meet in Heaven* by Mitch Albom. I brought *Undaunted Courage*, an introduction to the Lewis and Clark expedition of the Louisiana Purchase by Stephen Ambrose.

Cramped in coach between two passengers, I lowered the table on the back of the seat in front of me and pulled out a notebook and pen. I reflected on my past military life and thought back several months when Tim had emailed from the BRIDGE in reply to an email I had sent him in which I bellyached about my lack of opportunity to get educated in the U.S. Army forty-two years ago. Unlike my care less attitude when I served (1961-1964), Tim had an optimistic outlook and a positive sense of unselfish pride with his Navy rating as an Engineman. His forward-thinking mindset supported his lively sense of achievement, and to my delight he expressed enthusiastic gratitude for the opportunity to become educated while serving on active duty, an opportunity not offered by the military when I served during the Cold War in West Germany.

I got up to stretch my legs and hung around the rear emergency exit, gazing out the portal at a long white streak on the surface of the ocean: the trailing wake of a seagoing ship. As the reflection of the water sparkled up and peeked through the clouds that drifted by, I thought about the last time I had seen Tim: seventeen months ago at his recruit training graduation in front of the great water fountain in Grant Park, downtown Chicago. Things had changed since then. He was now a father; moreover, he had served his country with honor in time of war.

MY EARS POPPED when the plane descended to the Hawaiian archipelago, a chain of ancient seamounts created by the movement of the Pacific plate over a hot spot on the ocean floor. I surveyed the volcanic islands while the Boeing 737 dipped its wing as it approached. From several thousand feet above the island, Oahu was remarkably green. Its weatherworn mountains were deeply ribbed and beautifully sculptured by the passage of time.

I stepped off the plane and wondered why I was still wearing cool weather clothes. I had worn a long sleeve shirt and a windbreaker for the chilly morning in Cleveland, but when the door swung open in Oahu, a warm wall of humidity reminded me that I was in the tropics.

Corrin set the pace on the concourse. It didn't take long to work up a mild sweat while we walked quickstep to the baggage area. She was several feet in front of me, but that wasn't new. She had always been one step ahead, even in high school where she lettered eight times: four in cheerleading and four in track.

My mind fired up when I saw the baggage area. Corrin glanced a sweet looking smile when she noticed my eyes tearing over, then shot me an all-knowing look, the kind that seemed to say, *I gotcha, Dad.* When we arrived, Tim was waiting near the conveyor in a short sleeve tropical shirt. He had lost his teenage look—a little heavier but trim. A broad smile brightened his face, which had the well-rounded look of manhood. Its shape reminded me of my sister Molly. His physique was one of strength: a good build and a broad chest. His hair was cropped short military style. He was taller, an unusual sight for me since my image of Tim had been from his teenage years when he was shorter than his sister. His taller, larger frame now dwarfed Corrin.

Tim released Corrin from a bear hug and threw his arms around me. I buried my face in the nape of his neck and smelled the sweet scent of tropical sweat and cigarette smoke on his shirt. I looped my arm around his upper back, cupping my hand on his shoulder. That's when I realized he was taller than me.

TIM GRABBED MY BAG and carried it to the Hertz shuttle. Without pausing, he talked all the way to the rental agency, where he climbed into the back seat of our SUV and continued telling stories of Navy life in the Persian Gulf. Military acronyms spewed from his lips in an unending stream of alphabet letters. Although Corrin sat in the front seat, she had turned nearly backwards facing Tim. I could feel her sense of fascination. When she pleaded for details about the Navy, I realized it was the first time I had ever heard my kids communicating as adults.

I had been to Oahu twice before and had seen its interesting geological formations on the eastern shore. I wanted my kids to see them, so I headed north across the spine of the island—the Koolau Mountain Range—and stopped on top at the Nuuanu Pali pass. The view from the sheer cliff was absolutely stunning from 1200 feet. The pass overlooked the western part of the island and the hazy Pacific Ocean in the distance. I looked out over the horizon and imagined a swarm of Japanese Zeros in attack formation on December 7, 1941.

Oahu Beach

We descended on a winding road to the foot of the mountain and headed for the black lava beaches with shallow tide pools teeming with life. Meandering around the eastern shoreline, where the volcanic mountain range tapered into the sea, we came to Hanauma Bay and decided to return in the morning to snorkel.

* * * * *

Wednesday, October 29

IT WAS 3:30 A.M. and I couldn't sleep. The daylight hours were especially long because of the five-hour time zone shift; Corrin was four hours difference; Tim was on Navy time. I had flown west *with* the sun, but my body clock hadn't changed. So I got out of bed. I kept my watch on eastern standard to keep track of time, knowing that when I got back to Cleveland, I had to make a thirty-six hour turnaround and fly east to Italy *against* the sun, six hours later.

I showered and shaved without waking the kids, then took the elevator downstairs to the open-air lobby where potted palms waved in the breeze. Across the street the yellow lights of Denny's restaurant beckoned. I felt a sense of time-out-of-place, so I wandered over and ordered a cup of Kona.

Looking around the dining room, I saw the "night owls" hanging around after closing down the bars. One sleepy drunk nodded out in an overstuffed booth while he waited for breakfast. His head slowly slumped and gently jerked, then snapped back, only to drift away again and again. When his pancakes and eggs finally arrived, he sat straight up—bright-eyed—as if he had been awake all along. I smiled and wondered how many times I had nodded out in a booth.

AN AMERICAN BLONDE WOMAN — After Corrin and Tim got up, we hurried off to the Naval base where the USS Bridge was moored next to the mighty flagship of the Fifth Fleet, the massive USS Nimitz, a nuclear powered aircraft carrier. Corrin and I officially checked in as Tigers on the BRIDGE and stowed our bags below, then rendezvoused with Tim on the main deck and headed back to town.

On my previous trips to Oahu, I had missed seeing the watery tomb of the USS Arizona, so we drove to the busy tourist site and waited an hour for a Navy launch to shuttle us to the site. A manicured lawn embraced by a low coral wall served as the outside waiting area for the crowd, and in the distance, moored like stately kings, were two warships: the USS Bridge and the USS Nimitz. I began to compose a photograph of Corrin and Tim with the ships in the background when an English speaking Japanese man, who was part of a tour group, offered to take the picture with me in it. I handed him my camera.

A few minutes later a second Japanese man who did not speak English approached Corrin. It seemed obvious by his actions that he wanted Corrin to take his picture with his camera. She giggled and reached for his camera, but he politely resisted and refused to hand it to her. Corrin bowed several times, pleading innocence with her pretty smile. He returned each of Corrin's bows, but even deeper. The two of them bowed back and forth like a couple of bobble head toys. The English speaking Japanese man finally walked over and translated on behalf of his friend, who wanted Corrin, an American blond woman, to be in the photograph *with* him.

"He has never seen a blond before," the translator chuckled. A burst of laughter exploded from Corrin, and her face flushed in a moment of fun. She posed with the gentleman while the English speaking man took their picture. But one picture was not enough. In the same way family members gather around a wedding photographer to take their own picture of the bride and groom, the other tourists stepped forward and photographed the American blond woman with their Japanese friend. Delighted with her new sense of celebrity, Corrin bathed in the limelight while the cameras clicked away.

Arizona Memorial

USS ARIZONA AND THE PUNCHBOWL — When the loudspeaker announced our scheduled boarding time, a Navy launch shuttled us out to the ARIZONA where we mingled in silence on an open-air platform above the sunken ship. In a quiet memorial room, the crowd stood motionless as they read the 1177 inscribed names on a large marble wall—the honor role—all of whom had perished in the huge explosion that ripped the USS Arizona and sent her to the bottom.

On the six-minute return trip, I thought about those who had died in the Pacific campaign during World War II. Many of them were buried in an ancient caldera known as the Punchbowl, the National Memorial Cemetery of the Pacific. We drove to the quiet cemetery with sloping sides ascending to its rim, thus forming the shape of a punchbowl. It held the remains of more than 35,000 sailors and soldiers.

Chinese banyan trees lined the winding roads around the cemetery like silent sentries, umbrella-like with light gray twisted limbs and trunks. A beautiful lawn carpeted the crater. Granite makers lying flush with the grass identified the graves of the fallen. Inside the main building hung photographs of Medal of Honor recipients. I felt sad and patriotic as I read the descriptions of their unselfish deeds.

Several hours later and back at the hotel, we freshened up and headed downstairs for happy hour. Under the warm shade of Royal palms rustling in the breeze on the patio, we toasted our reunion with Mai Tai cocktails laden with heavy spears of fresh fruit.

I leaned back and interlaced my fingers behind my head. "Tell us some more war stories, Tim."

"Yeah, Timmy," Corrin added. "Tell us about your life on the ship."

Tim started up again with entertaining anecdotes, and between munching the bar nuts and listening to the war stories, we laughed and blended as a family again. Several rounds of refreshments quickly went by, and we all got tight and a little bit high.

Corrin jumped up. "What'll we eat?" she said.

"Fish," I replied.

Tim agreed, but we wound up eating Chinese cuisine at the House of Hong. The food made us sleepy.

* * * * *

Thursday, October 30

BACK TO DENNY'S — The following morning I returned to Denny's for another pre-dawn breakfast of sausage and eggs. It was good to be awake and writing in my journal. After an hour, I finished off the last sip of coffee and headed for the door.

Outside, small groups of young adults lingered on the sidewalk in the warm night air. Pausing spontaneously in bursts of laughter, the fun-loving couples drifted slowly down the street—young Americans courting each other, looking for love. The men bellowed like bulls, while the women laughed and posed in their tropical form-fitting clothes. When a few of them embraced, I recalled my single life on the West Coast from 1966-72. I was twenty-three then and bellowed like a bull myself, you know, in the bars of Los Angeles. Ah, now *those* were the good old days.

When I got back to our room, Corrin was in the bathroom; Tim was still asleep. As soon as his sister finished with her shower, he got up. We grabbed a cup of coffee and spent the second morning swimming inside an ancient volcano crater on the eastern shore of Oahu: Hanauma Bay. Millenniums ago, one of its sides gave way to the pounding sea and formed a secluded shallow bay. For centuries it had been reserved for Hawaii's royal family, but it was now a nature preserve. By 8:30 a.m. we had rented equipment and were snorkeling in the tepid salty water. A number of colorful fish made their homes in the shallow coral reefs near the shore, including a four-foot shark that lingered in a coral cove on the sandy bottom directly below where we treaded water and watched.

We returned to our room and showered, packed our bags, headed for the rental agency, and dropped off the car. Hertz shuttled us to the airport USO, where military buses waited to transfer sailors to the base.

When we arrived, security was strict at the front gate, but we passed onto the pier without a hitch, except for a blaring bullhorn command from a shore patrol police boat motoring in the water near the gate. As I raised my camera to photograph the NIMITZ, a demanding voice boomed over the loudspeaker: "No photographs allowed!" Humbled and embarrassed in front of my children, I lowered my head and slunk away, affirming my compliance with the policeman's order with a firm nod of my head. Tim and Corrin looked at me in silence.

Considering the length of an aircraft carrier, the two ships straddled a very long pier. In a huge shadow cast by the BRIDGE, Corrin and I rubbernecked our way down the pier, following Tim between the ships. When we arrived midway, I looked through a large opening in the side of the

Bridge & Nimitz Pearl Harbor

carrier—a work bay filled with forklifts and sailors. Turning to the brow (gangway) of our ship, we climbed forty-two steps to the main deck and met the Tiger welcoming committee.

Following an abbreviated tour below deck, and after Tim took care of some business, we returned to the security gate and left the base. Just beyond the gate was an open-air tent packed with sailors raising plastic beer cups, delighted to be back on American soil. Officers and enlisted personnel casually kicked back and shared the same tables, drinking libations they had very little of at sea. The BRIDGE had carried a limited supply of beer for the crew, which was rationed at two cans each, but only after the ship had been out to sea for forty-four days without a liberty call.

DINNER AT SAM SNEAD'S TAVERN — After an hour of social drinking in the tent, Tim's shipmate came by. Petty Officer First Class Pete Knight had Tigers onboard too. They joined us at a local golf course for supper at Sam Snead's Tavern. After several rounds of Crown Royal, Tim became animated as he told us war stories. He led the group in laughter, followed by Corrin, who drank Tim's drink of choice and added to the fun.

The dinner party rolled on in riotous laughter, but 8:00 p.m. was 1:00 a.m. Cleveland time. Corrin and I needed to organize our personal effects and prepare for our stay on ship, so we called a taxi and headed back.

FIRST NIGHT ON SHIP — A red soft glow bathed the sleeping quarters twenty-four hours a day. Low wattage light bulbs provided just enough light to dress, yet were dim enough to sleep. Since many of the returning sailors took shore leave in Hawaii, their beds were empty and available for

Tigers to use. I slept in Tim's bunk while he made his own bed on a makeshift mattress in the Cargo Fuels laboratory where he and his crewmates were known to spend time and sack out.

Dressed in my socks and a pair of blue pajamas I had layered over my underwear, I prepared for a cool night. Since the bunks were three beds high, and I was on the top, I needed to climb up to get into bed each night. Using my right foot, I located then stepped into a narrow built-in pocket foothold in the bulkhead, but climbing with my right foot was wrong. I should have used my "other" right. Bunks on the left side where I slept required the left foot to climb; bunks on the right required the right foot. When I mounted using my right foot, I swung my left knee to the bed, but it struck the bulkhead. Now, stuck in that position with no room to maneuver my knee or switch feet in the narrow pocket, I had to get down and remount using my left foot.

Finally atop my bunk, I had to wrestle with two cotton blankets. No matter what I did, I could not cover myself properly. I kicked and pushed and flipped the blankets with my feet. Nothing worked. Frustrated, I finally sat up. Being on top bunk, however, I had the headroom to sit up, but Corrin did not, as I found out the next day when she reported being sandwiched between two bunks with the same problem. She couldn't sit up. When she woke in the morning, she was twisted and tangled inside her blankets. Deciding to ditch the blankets, Corrin kept warm with three layers of tee shirts and the hood of her sweatshirt tied tightly around her head.

Correcting my unruly blankets, as I sat in bed, I pulled them up and folded them one at a time, twice over, corners meeting, until they formed a rectangle the same width as the bed. In the morning I folded them accordion style and placed them at the foot of the bed, making them ready for the next night.

I settled down on my back, turned on the overhead reading lamp behind my head, and looked at Tim's photographs taped to the bulkhead inches from my face. It had been eight months since he had seen his wife, and he had never seen his first child but for email pictures on the wall.

A constant stream of cool air blew against the top of my head, so I propped up a pillow against it. While I lay in the dark, I wondered about Corrin's first night in the women's quarters. She could take care of herself. After all, she had lived in the student dormitories of Miami University and with travelers in the youth hostels of Europe. Navy living would add to that experience, the kind of experience she never would have gotten but for a Tiger Cruise on a United States Navy warship.

* * * * *

Friday, October 31

CHOW CALL — It was 4:00 a.m. and quiet. I had a routine by then. Each morning I sat in the galley with my journal and wrote about the day before. Although no food was served at that early hour, there was plenty of hot coffee, peanut butter, and bread.

Chow call rang out at 6:00 a.m. along with the sound of clinking pots and pans echoing off the stainless steel in the kitchen. The aroma of warm breakfast food wafted through the galley. I was the first one in line when the steam table opened. At first, I wondered if Navy chow was the same as it was in the U.S. Army forty-two years ago. It was.

I dipped a long-handle serving spoon into a large pot of steaming hot oatmeal and piled a plop into my bowl. Since I got the first scoop, the pat of melting butter on top was mine. Hot cakes and sweet syrup were next, followed by bacon, sausage, and eggs.

"How do you want your eggs, sir?" a cook in a white apron asked.

"Over easy, please."

"Yes, sir," he snapped.

I topped off my tray with a piece of fresh fruit and a container of yogurt, then headed for the toaster—white and wheat, raisin and rye, bagels and butter and jelly. The metal conveyor chains in the two commercial toasters carried the bread slices past the heating elements and dropped them into a tray, a production line of toast. Just what the Navy needed, I thought. Two large coffee urns supplied the caffeine. Packets of hot chocolate and tea bags sat nearby. If you were still hungry, you got back into line.

THE USS BRIDGE SHOVES OFF — At 1000 hours the BRIDGE shoved off. Clouds of churning sand wallowed up while tugboat propellers worked to push the ship away from the pier. Ever so slowly, and with increasing momentum, the mighty BRIDGE floated away from the pier and into the channel. Escorted by the pair of tugboats, the ship sailed slowly under its own power through Pearl Harbor, passing the USS Arizona Memorial and the *Mighty Mo*, the USS Missouri, a World War II battleship moored close by. An incoming submarine slid into the harbor and passed us on our port side. Its cigar-like profile cut a rippled, v-shaped wake in the water, and upon its deck stood a long line of sailors at parade rest. The crews on both ships snapped to attention and saluted each other at the sound of the ship's whistle. Goosebumps formed on the back of my neck as the ships passed. When we cleared the mouth of the harbor, the BRIDGE was underway.

The vivid turquoise water off the coast of Oahu changed to opalescent green when we hit the open sea. Breaking waves from the ship's bow churned the ocean air into white-crested waves, and from my perspective looking down from the signal bridge, the colors intensified. Billowing puffs of white clouds floated on the wide horizon. The tropical sun beat down its heated rays and cast cool shadows across the steel gray decks of the BRIDGE.

By 1100 hours the USS Ruben James followed in our wake. It positioned itself to our stern port side for an underway fuel replenishment, the first of many demonstrations on the Tiger Cruise. In Navy jargon fuel replenishment was known as an *unrep*. Although there were fuel line riggings strung between the two ships, no fuel was actually transferred. It was a dry run for the crews. After completing its mission, the RUBEN JAMES returned to Pearl Harbor, but within the hour a cruiser, the USS Princeton, pulled alongside for another unrep, but this time fuel was transferred.

Petty Officer Third Class Richards controlled the transfer of fuel from a sophisticated console in Cargo Fuels, the command center for the dispersement of JP-5 jet and marine diesel fuels. Although originally assigned to Engineering/Air Conditioning and Refrigeration Division, EN3(SW) Richards was temporarily reassigned when a petty officer in charge of fuel dispersement was called home on emergency leave. Tim was selected by his superiors to replace the petty officer and assumed responsibility during replenishment operations in the Persian Gulf, where he personally transferred over 93 million gallons

Cargo Fuels Control Room

of fuel and 30,000 gallons of potable water to coalition ships during *Operation Iraqi Freedom.*

USS NIMITZ (CVN-68) — Following the refueling operation of the USS Princeton, the ship dropped back and remained in formation, while we waited for the nuclear powered USS Nimitz to appear. Lead ship of its class and flagship of the Fifth Fleet, the NIMITZ approached in our wake and gradually pulled up along our port side—160 feet away!—and matched its speed with the speed of the BRIDGE. As the two warships sliced through the water, their bows cut a narrow channel of turbulence between them, the force of which created powerful waves that ran at oblique angles and crashed with great force against each other.

The massive aircraft carrier stretched 1090 feet, had a 134-foot beam, and with a flight deck measuring 252 feet wide, it dominated the scene. If I live another hundred years, I don't think I will ever see a sight so captivating and awe-inspiring as the USS Nimitz sailing 160 feet away. And the demonstration had just begun.

HIGH-LINE TRANSFER — From my elevated position on the signal bridge, I still had to look up to the landing deck of the aircraft carrier, which served as a viewing platform for a large crowd of civilian Tigers and Navy personnel waiting for the high-line show to begin.

When I heard the crack of a modified M-14 rifle fire a weighted leader line across to the BRIDGE, I saw a detail of sailors pick it up and attach it to another larger line. A wench pulled it back to the NIMITZ. That line was connected to another larger line, and, in turn, that line was pulled back to the

BRIDGE and connected to another larger line. Eventually the largest of the lines brought back a steel high-line cable that swung between the ships. The cable was attached to a hydraulic mechanism in the side opening of the carrier, where Admiral Locklear and his personal aide appeared in hardhats and life jackets. Dangling in an open-air two-man seat that swung wildly in the wind, the two officers transferred to the BRIDGE, while white-tipped waves snapped at their feet.

A few minutes before the transfer began, I had overheard Captain Stockton briefing his staff. In a sober tone he reminded them that the high-line transfer was "not a good time to tea-bag-dunk the admiral."

Following an award ceremony honoring Captain Stockton, winner of the Arleigh Burke Fleet Trophy, Admiral Locklear returned to the NIMITZ in the same manner he arrived. The admiral's showboating reminded me of a well-publicized event earlier that year when President George W. Bush landed on USS Abraham Lincoln aircraft carrier in the Persian Gulf. A little showboating by the commander-in-chief was a heart-warming highlight of *Operation Iraqi Freedom.*

HALLOWEEN NIGHT in the galley was not a trick, but a treat. There was a cash prize for the best costume, which was judged by two petty officers dressed as women in combat boots and wigs.

Each contestant had to act out his costume character to be eligible for the prize. There was a lot of camaraderie and fun.

Another cash contest involved the ship's cook. He prepared a disgusting pot of green goo made from chow line leftovers. Barbie Doll parts were disassembled and thrown into the large pot, and each contestant had two minutes to reach in, stir around, and search for Barbie's parts. Corrin was up to her elbow in the slime and held first place with five parts, but got beat out when another Tiger won by an "arm's" length.

* * * * *

Saturday, November 1

SHIP TOURS BEGAN today. Tigers assembled with the crew for morning work call and divided into small groups. Assigned as a tour leader for the engine room, Petty Officer Richards took our group down into the *main space* where four huge turbine engines, along with auxiliary cooling equipment, evaporators, and boilers were housed. To make room inside the ship for the enormous machinery, several inside decks were cut away—no ceilings—just walkways, platforms, and steep staircases.

The noise in the main space was deafening. Although Tim did not wear his earplugs in the engine room, Corrin and I quickly plugged our ears. It was so loud that a padded soundproof telephone booth had a light mounted on its side. It flashed brightly, alerting the crew when the telephone rang.

And it was hot down there—very hot—a dry kind of heat.

THE AIR SHOW — The afternoon demonstration of military muscle began when the USS Princeton fired several rounds into the ocean from its five-inch deck gun. I waited for a guided missile to launch, but no such luck. Once the PRINCETON had completed its mission, it dropped back in formation and followed in our wake.

Shortly afterwards, the USS Nimitz appeared on our aft port side and made ready for the next demonstration: helicopters and "superman" sailors.

Two UH-46D Boeing SeaKnight helicopters demonstrated their versatility as they rose from the landing deck of the NIMITZ and whirled around the three ships. One of the helicopters returned to the NIMITZ, hovered over the landing deck, and picked up three sailors who were attached to a steel cable, stacked ten feet apart. They were lifted ladder-like off the deck and flown around the ships, hanging freely in the wind on the cable. As the SeaKnight circled the area several times, the dangling sailors looked as if they were supermen with their arms and legs outstretched, forming the letters X.

Navy pilots in fighter jets were next. They roared by in spectacular fashion, executing aerial maneuvers for the crowd. One of them leveled off slightly higher than the super structure of the

NIMITZ. It passed by so quickly that I had difficulty keeping the aircraft in my camera viewfinder. Silence followed—then a thunderous sonic boom.

"Yesss!" I cried out, clinching my fist. Other Tigers standing near me shook their heads, dropped their jaws, and opened their eyes with amazement.

BOMB RUNS — One of several bomb runs began when a fighter jet released multiple bombs on a smoking target floating on the water. Pressure waves from the explosions reached us a few seconds after plumbs of gray smoke appeared on the ocean surface.

The final bomb run looked like a ballet. A one-ton piece of ordnance dropped from the jet, but unlike the World War II movies where hundreds of bombs seem to drop vertically to the ground, this military  bad boy flew through the air like a long white cigar, its trajectory curving perfectly to its target. A huge plumb of gray matter erupted over the water when it exploded, and it took several seconds before its thunderous clap reached our ears.

The next show demonstrated the transfer of jet fuel from one plane to another. It reminded me of two dragonflies mating in flight. Afterward, a surveillance plane appeared with a radar disk mounted on top of its fuselage. The plane dipped its wing towards us to present a better view as it flew by.

The final event of the afternoon featured sixteen aircraft assembled in crosshatch formation flying high above the ships. Great whoops erupted from the crowd as they passed over us. I felt proud to be an American and privileged to have been invited on a United States Navy Tiger Cruise.

* * * * *

Sunday, November 2

A PRIVATE TOUR — On Sunday morning the ship's chaplain, Lieutenant Edward "Chaps" Bass, conducted a Protestant service in the galley. We sang twelve hymns, none of which I knew. Two sailors witnessed in front of a small congregation of twelve people. One of them was thankful for having quit smoking. There was no sermon that morning; Chaplin Bass apologized. The galley had to be cleared by 1000 hours.

Tiger tours continued after church, but this time Petty Officer Richards gave Corrin and me a private tour of some of the ship's remaining compartments. He walked us through several huge refrigerators, known as *reefers* in Navy lingo. Although they were empty after eight months at sea, the reefers had held millions of dollars worth of groceries and perishable goods, which were distributed throughout 190 U.S. and Coalition warships in support of *Operation Iraqi Freedom.*

It was a good thing we were athletic. Tim led us from deck to deck, maneuvering quickly through a maze of narrow passageways, rectangular hatches, vertical wall ladders, and steep staircases. When I descended the stairs between decks (facing forward), only the heels of my shoes connected with the narrow steel

Tim & Corrin tour the engine room

steps. Each time I used a staircase—up or down—I had to focus on what I was doing. Otherwise I could strike my forehead against the bulkhead, which I did more than once. And steel plate is hard. Corrin acquired three distinct bruises on her legs from catching her shins on the airlock doorframes as she stepped over them.

Tim took us back down to the main space, but unlike the day before when Tigers got a cursory overview of the engine room, he gave us a thorough tour, pointing out in elaborate detail the working mechanisms of the powerful equipment that supported the crew and propelled the ship. With a 107-foot beam, the BRIDGE had plenty of space to house its massive propulsion plants, specifically: four General Electric LM2500 gas turbine engines, each generating 26,500 pounds of shaft horsepower, the equivalent of four DC-10 jet engines. The look of amazement came over Corrin's face while Tim described the operation of the equipment. His professional understanding of the engineering aspects of the ship's mechanical systems was remarkable. I could tell he was in his element.

We followed Tim down to the bowels of the boat: deck seven. About thirty feet above us—the ship had a thirty-nine foot draft (full)—I heard the sound of waves crashing against the bulkhead. Only Noah was lower than us, I thought. Tim pointed to a hatch on the floor and opened it, deck eight, the bottom of the boat. In the small room below us was a metal device protruding through the bottom of the hull that registered the speed of the ship.

BERTHING QUARTERS — I began getting ready for bed at 6:00 p.m., which was 11:00 p.m. Cleveland time. In the dim lit sleeping quarters, I saw dark blue ball caps embossed with the ship's crest hanging over blue denim work uniforms that hung on hooks. Scuffed leather boots and shower room flip-flops lay scattered along the bulkheads. Beds were hastily made. Laundry bags bulged. Bath towels draped and dried wherever they were hung. I felt right at home in the clustered sleeping quarters of the BRIDGE. Unlike the two-man Army bunks and the olive drab footlockers that lined up straighter than an arrow when I was stationed at Fort Knox, Kentucky, Navy ship berthing was a lot less formal and a lot more cluttered.

My berthing section had six beds, each with a horizontal locking drawer. Each stack of three was separated by thirty-six inches of floor space and constructed of two steel racks assembled three bunks high. The only way for me to get off the top bunk was to muster up my athletic ability. I pushed back my horizontal privacy curtain, and in the same manner as an orangutan, I stretched out my left arm and grabbed the rigid light fixture that hung between the two racks. With my right hand, I grabbed the rigid curtain bar. Then with a swift muscular movement from a position on my back, I sprung with my hips, pulled with my arms, and flipped sideways into space, hanging for a moment until my toes touched the deck. It was not easy getting out of bed to use the *head* in the middle of the night.

The head had five small sinks, which lined up side by side beneath a horizontal mirror of highly polished metal. In its reflection I saw four private toilet stalls, and off to my left was a narrow shower room with three curtained stalls. The head was compact and clean, and other than the engine room and kitchen, it was the only place onboard that was warm.

There was plenty of hot water, and strong pressure provided a soothing neck massage, making my morning showers a pleasure. But drying off in the cramped wet shower room was a bit tight. When I dried my feet and flip-flops, I had to lean against the bulkhead to balance myself; there was no place to sit. I tried sitting in the adjoining dayroom on a steel seat, but I only did that once. It was ice cold; so was the air. The constant breeze from the ventilation system made the dayroom just as drafty as the rest of the ship.

I stuffed my laundry bag with dirty clothes and noticed my Fruit of the Loom was missing. I doubled back to the head and found it on the floor. The next morning I found my soap dish where I had left it—in the shower stall.

I wondered how Corrin was doing with her morning routine. I laughed when she told me she had dropped her clean panties on the wet floor as she headed for the shower. When she finished washing, she had to leave the warm room and walk quickly through the cold air in a damp towel and dripping hair to retrieve a clean pair from her suitcase.

THE SHIP'S INTERIOR — There were hundreds of locking hatches, many of which were pressurized, separating one watertight compartment from the next. We passed through them on a regular basis. I called it the airlock drill. To enter a pressurized airlock, I lifted and threw counter-clockwise the twenty-inch steel bar that broke the seal on the door. Whoosh. Then I snapped open the spring-loaded safety latch above the bar and pulled open the hatch. I stepped over the high doorframe into the small, pressurized compartment, then repeated the same procedure and locked the hatch behind me. I turned around and repeated the procedure a third time as I exited. After all the clanging, banging, and ear-popping, I turned and closed the hatch, reaching up to relock the spring-loaded safety latch, after I threw the twenty-inch steel bar for the last time.

All metal surfaces were painted except stainless steel, and there was plenty of that. Black arrows stenciled on color-coded pipes indicated the direction of flow. The interior of the ship was a mystifying maze of steel hatches, colored pipes, and bundled wires. There had to be at least 120 hatches on the ship, 100 times that number for pipes, and 500 times the number of pipes for wires! And everything was identified.

Here is a quiz: What is the common name for the following identification plate? 1-552-1-DK-WR&WC-1-551-1-L. You may have guessed it: a toilet/washbasin room.

A COOL SPOT IN THE GALLEY — The constant breeze from the air conditioning system was chilly. One morning in the galley I ribbed Tim and his friends about the temperature at the table where we ate. Everyday, most of them sat in the same place, directly in line with a cool breeze that turned my sausage cold—real cold. When I suggested we move to a different table, the sailors rolled their eyes and laughed. Tim humored me and explained about the intense heat of the Persian Gulf where the air temperature reached 110 degrees in the summer, and the water in which they floated was 90. The ship simply heated up; so did the crew. The cool spot in the galley was a refuge from that heat.

But solidified sausage grease was too much for me, so I moved my tray and found a warmer spot, if I could call it that. Each morning, dressed in a windbreaker and a crested USS Bridge ball cap, I returned to the same "warm" spot to write my journal. It was peaceful at 4:00 a.m., and the hum of the air conditioning system acted as white noise, a background sound that helped me concentrate on writing.

Galley

CATASTROPHIC FAILURES — Petty Officer Richards had an excellent reputation on board as a trouble-shooter. He also had a *can do* attitude that "saved the ship" when two of its four 250-ton air conditioning units failed. Needless to say, air conditioning had a high priority in the hot water of the Persian Gulf. With two broken units, the ship quickly heated up. Tim accomplished what other enginemen could not: he repaired the units and got them running at a cool 39 degrees. His ability and willingness to do the job, along with several other important accomplishments, earned him the Navy and Marine Corps Medal of Achievement. In appreciation of Tim's outstanding performance, his crewmates nicknamed him after the popular cartoon character, the nerdy genius Jimmy Neutron.

It took Tim's section chief eight years to earn his medal of achievement, the same one Tim earned in twenty months.

Corrin & Tim & Tim

* * * * *

Monday, November 3

PETTY OFFICER RICHARDS EARNS A MEDAL — Award ceremonies were held this morning. Sailors mustered on deck and stood at attention as the master chief read the citations of a select group of men and women whose accomplishments were recognized. Most of the sailors earned certificates, but Tim was among a small number who earned a medal. Recipients stood straight face while their citations were read, except Tim. For a brief moment a flashing smile burst across his face as his section chief pinned the medal[4] on his uniform.

SEA WHIZ — The afternoon schedule was packed with activities. Tiger demonstrations began with a tour of one of the ship's self-defense mechanisms: the MK 15 Phalanx Close-In Weapons System (CIWS). Although the acronym was pronounced "sea whiz," many sailors had nicknamed the Phalanx "R2-D2" because of the shape of its radar dome. It resembled the mechanical droid from the movie *Star Wars*.

Corrin & Sea Whiz

[4] Department of the Navy: This is to certify that the Secretary of the Navy has awarded the Navy and Marine Crops Achievement Medal to Engineman Third Class (Surface Warfare) Timothy F. Richards, United States Navy, for professional achievement while serving as auxiliaries technician and repair part petty officer on board USS Bridge (AOE 10), while deployed to Fifth Fleet in support of Operations Enduring Freedom and Iraqi Freedom from March 2003 to August 2003. Displaying superb technical abilities, Petty Officer Richards skillfully repaired and maintained fan coil units, laundry steam presses, crew washers and dryers, ice machines, refrigerators, scullery and various other galley equipment, resulting in excellent shipboard quality of life. His extensive technical knowledge and expertise were instrumental in the timely repair of two 250-ton air conditioning units. Demonstrating uncommon motivation, he expeditiously procured critical repair parts for five work centers, contributing directly to superior material condition and operational readiness. Petty Officer Richards reflected great credit on himself and upheld the high traditions on the United States Naval Service. Given this 15th day of August 2003. For the Secretary of the Navy, R.V. Stockton, Captain, U.S. Navy, Commanding Officer USS Bridge (AOE 10)

The MK 15 Phalanx was a fast reaction rapid-fire 20-millimeter gun system designed to engage anti-ship cruise missiles and fixed-wing aircraft. It consisted of a combination of radars, computers, and multiple rapid-fire M61A1 Vulcan 6-barreled cannon. The Gatling-style gun, with its rotating cluster of barrels, was capable of firing either 3000 or 4500 rounds per minute with a burst length of continuous 60 or 100 rounds.

Six Tigers showed up for the live fire demonstration on the starboard side of the ship and stood about twenty-five feet from the gun. It occurred to me after hearing the rapid explosions why the mechanism had also been nicknamed "sea whiz." When fired, the continuous thundering noise made a high-pitched whizzzzzzzzzz. The detonations at twenty-five feet away were painful, and following each two-second burst I felt a hard ache inside my head. Four bursts over the open water were too much for me, an ache too painful to bear. So I went below to the Cargo Fuels section room seeking silence and a couple of aspirin. My ears rang for hours.

M2 MACHINE GUN — I hooked up with Corrin for the next demonstration then headed for the stern of the ship. Located one deck below the helicopter flight deck was a Browning .50 (inch) caliber machine gun mounted on a side rail overlooking the peaceful Pacific. The fully automatic machine gun fired 12.7-millimeter shells at a rate of 550 rounds per minute. Each shell exploded with a heavy thud. First produced in 1932 as a vehicle weapon, the M2 had been heavily utilized during World War II, the Korean War, the Vietman Conflict, as well as operations in Afghanistan and Iraq in the 1990s and 2000s.

Again, I was reminded of my U.S. Army days. On a field training exercise with the 35th Artillery Group, 37th Artillery, in Grafenwoehr, Germany, I was the assigned operator of an armored personnel carrier (APC) that had a .50 caliber machine gun mounted on its turret. Sitting in the driver's seat equipped with a range finder periscope, I sat beneath a closed hatch with my face securely planted against a heavily padded eyepiece and fired the weapon.

The two sailors in charge of the M2 gun site issued instructions to don a flak jacket and put on a protective helmet. I complied, and after firing several bursts over the open water, I collected a few brass casings from the deck and thanked the crewmen. While Corrin fired off a few bursts of her own, I wandered over to the designated smoking area on the stern and was reminded of Tim's recruit training at Great Lakes, Illinois, where recruits were not allowed to smoke during basic training. But the sailors on the BRIDGE were not recruits.

SEAKNIGHT HELICOPTER — Corrin and I climbed a steep staircase to the flight deck, which served a multiple purpose. The deck was large enough for a steel beach picnic, outdoor movies at night, and, of course, helicopter liftoffs. To get a better view of the action on the flight deck, we climbed up two additional *levels* to watch the flight crew prepare a UH-46D SeaKnight helicopter for take off.

After carefully following pre-launch procedures, the crewman signaled the pilots, who engaged the rotary transmission and lifted off. Rising above the deck with its whirling blades, the aircraft hovered about seventy-five feet off the stern, where it maintained a forward speed equal to the speed of the ship.

Suddenly the helicopter whirled around and pointed at us—nose down, tail up. It hovered in a menacing manner, like a glassy-eyed insect might pose for a kill. Although the SeaKnight was not designed to carry assault weapons, the pilots seemed to be "aiming" at us. Tigers signaled thumbs up and gave the pilots several rounds of rousing cheers when they tipped the aircraft back and forth and rocked it side to side. If you wore a hat, you held on to it; the backwash was strong. The SeaKnight departed and waited about a half mile away, while the crew got ready for the next demonstration.

Tim J & helicopter

OPEN WATER RESCUE — A light breeze blew out of the south. Ocean swells were small. The BRIDGE slowed down and stopped, but kept its engines running. Tigers gathered along the starboard side and watched three sailors in an inflatable rubber boat—the Zodiac type that oceanographer Jacques Cousteau used for his ocean expeditions. While the men in the boat waited for the rescue helicopter to arrive, the driver revved the outboard engine and zoomed around in playful circles and figure eights.

The operation began when one of the sailors dressed in a wet suit jumped overboard. He acted as a casualty and waited in the water to be rescued. When the helicopter arrived, a rescue swimmer jumped from the aircraft and plunged about ten feet to the ocean. Obviously athletic, he sprinted towards the casualty with powerful arm strokes and leg kicks that churned the water like a Mississippi paddleboat. After assisting the casualty into a safety harness that was lowered from above, the swimmer signaled the helicopter to lift the rescue sling. Once the casualty was safely onboard, the sling was lowered back to the water for the swimmer.

Damage control was next. Tigers relaxed in the open air and watched the crew set up demonstration equipment on the flight deck.

DAMAGE CONTROL procedures were utilized to save the ship. Well-trained specialists assisted Tigers and explained the methods the crew used to put out fires, rescue people in smoke-filled compartments, and stop floodwater from entering the ship.

Controlling a high-pressure fire hose was not easy, even with three of us holding on. I put on

a welder's mask and cut through a piece of steel bulkhead with a cutting torch, the same way a damage control specialist might cut away battle wreckage or weld steel plates over flood holes in a bulkhead.

A smoke-filled room adjacent to one of the helicopter bays was set up to extract a casualty. Corrin and I volunteered for the demonstration.

Each of us strapped on a bulky oxygen tank and covered our faces with masks. Although Corrin was only an arm's length away from me, the dense smoke in the room obliterated the outline of her body. But two sailors guided us through the exercise, and one of them held up an electronic device through which we viewed the thermo, ghostlike image of a sailor lying on the floor about ten feet away.

When darkness fell over the Pacific Ocean, Captain Stockton met us on level three near the bridge—levels go up and decks go down. He carried a snub nose shotgun-like flare gun under his arm. Taking turns, we fired flares into the night sky and watched as their sparkling rays reflected off the ocean waves. The flares burst with eye-catching brilliance, drifted away on parachutes, then slowly descended to the water and went out. After each of us had several turns with the gun, Captain Stockton fired off the remaining shells in rapid succession. It was the 4th of July in November.

THANKSGIVING CAME EARLY — Captain Stockton decided to celebrate Thanksgiving three weeks early, so the galley cooks basted lots of turkeys and served all the holiday trimmings. The galley officer and kitchen crew decorated the mess hall with festive cardboard cutouts and a cornucopia of fresh fruit. I was impressed with the family-like atmosphere created by the crew's attention to detail. After dinner the galley cleared out for game night.

GAME NIGHT was a fun-filled evening of camaraderie, karaoke, and good old-fashioned fun. The spirit of the crowd was best described in the following article of "The Haze Gray," the ship's newsletter. ET3(SW) Cayce Smith wrote:

"Everyone Wants to Be a Superstar: A roomful of people, a couple of microphones, and a sound system; add a few brave souls with superstar ambition and you have yourself a party! The Tigers and crew got their grooves on with some good ole karaoke! People of all ages stepped up to the mike to cover everything from rock-n-roll to gospel and hip-hop to country. I can note that the XO, Commander Weedon's Elvis impersonation was overshadowed when BM3 Rose jumped up to the mike and wowed the audience with his dead-on recital of *Can't Help Falling in Love with You*. And of course, there were those two girls….Oh wait, that was ET2 Delgado and myself that rewrote the lyrics to *I Will Survive*. That song brought the house to its feet. There were many great performances, too many to list here, but the important thing is that everyone was entertained and had a great time!"

* * * * *

Tuesday, November 4

FIELD DAY — Tomorrow the sailors would be home, so the crew got busy cleaning the ship. Every compartment, every staircase, every passageway and section room got cleaned. Some sailors stood on ladders and wiped away the accumulated dust from the overhead pipes and air ducts. One lonely man bundled in warm clothing against the cold wind, sat silently next to the ship's weatherworn bell on the bow. As he patiently rubbed the brass surface in a series of little circles, chemically treated cotton balls dissolved away the accumulated tarnish. The job must have taken hours to complete.

KNOT TYING — By midmorning Tigers had assembled on deck for a knot-tying class; however, only one deckhand served as the instructor, and he was not a teacher. He only *showed* us what he knew. With a flash of his hand and a flip of a rope, he whipped up a couple of impressive looking knots, then gave each of us a length of rope with which to practice. The instructor could not handle the class of forty. Even so, we turned to each other for assistance in our meager attempt at tying knots.

Following a tasty lunch of tacos, enchiladas, and burritos, Tigers met with their sponsors for the ship's photo shoot. A few days earlier, several individuals had painted a mural of a jungle tiger on the inside bulkhead of deck one. It served as the backdrop for the Tiger Cruise souvenir photograph.

STEEL BEACH PICNIC — Beneath a canopy of blue skies, a warm ocean breeze embraced us, while galley personnel prepared a steel beach picnic for the crew and assembled outdoor cooking equipment on the flight deck. While pop music piped over the public-address system, hundreds of hotdogs and hamburgers huddled over a smoldering bed of charcoal on a huge grill. The usual picnic condiments and side dishes were served. Ice-covered cans of soda filled a huge, tub-like container.

In the evening the First Class Petty Officer Association generously gave away cold cash to celebrate the last night at sea. It was Big Buck$ Bingo night. It turned out to be very popular with civilians and sailors alike, but not enough seats were available in the galley to accommodate the crowd. Many sailors sat on the floor or leaned against the bulkhead. The big prizewinner of the evening was Brandon Crockwell, an eleven-year old Tiger who won the $2,000 grand prize!

Steel Beach Picnic

* * * * *

Wednesday, November 5

STRAIT OF JUAN DE FUCA — The brisk morning air swirled around my face when we entered the Juan de Fuca Strait at 0530 hours. I was already topside and looking at the first sighting of land: Canada on the left, the United States on the right. Tears streamed back alongside my temples as I stood in the cold morning wind and watched an oil tanker overtake us on our port side.

A beautiful dawn greeted the BRIDGE. The early morning hues served as a scenic backdrop of glowing color that silhouetted the coastal mountains. The lush landscape and gently rising mountains of the Northwest were beautiful at that time of the morning. Although the weather in the Seattle area was often rainy, foggy, or misty, it was not that morning. The yellow sun smiled warmly in the southern sky, while deep shadows lay low in contrast to brightly lit mountainsides covered with evergreens. Picturesque inlets and scattered homes lined the silent seashore.

From his position on the bridge overlooking the strait, Captain Stockton spotted a pod of killer whales approaching on the port side. They followed each other in formation, sleek and smooth, surfacing and diving as they passed our ship on their way out to sea. Their black and white markings easily identified them as they broke the surface of the water again and again. A few minutes later nature treated us again with a showing of sea lions on the starboard side.

BREMERTON NAVAL BASE — It seemed to take an unusual amount of time to arrive at Bremerton Naval Base, nearly eight hours from the time we entered the strait. Much of that time, however, was spent sailing at slow speed through the calm waters of the Juan de Fuca Strait and the Puget Sound. When we finally arrived at the Naval base, two tugboats greeted us in the harbor in front of our pier. One of them nudged up to us and allowed a harbor pilot to climb aboard. He assumed command of the docking operation.

A wide security net blocked the entrance to our pier. Its metal curtain draped beneath the surface of the water and stretched across the opening of the berth. The BRIDGE waited at a dead stop while the harbor police boats pulled back the net. Then the tugboats slowly maneuvered our stern until the ship was parallel with the pier—a ninety-degree turn. While we waited nearly thirty minutes for the ship to complete its turn, I listened to the distant muffled sound of a cheering crowd on the pier.

HOMECOMING — Sounds of busy sailors filled the air. Hundreds of them moved around on the main deck. Eager seamen and sea women dressed in Navy blues scurried about and lined up on the port side overlooking the pier. They were decked out in winter uniforms with white Dixie cup hats. All ranks of sailors tended to detail.

"Are my ribbons straight?" I overheard one of them ask. "How do I look?" They all looked good—crisp and clean from forward to aft. Standing at parade rest along the rail, they scanned the pier, trying to catch a glimpse of their loved ones waiting below.

"Where's Tim?" Corrin asked.

"I don't know."

Swiftly, we moved to the stern and found him standing in formation with his division. We fell in behind him and stayed close.

"Timmy, can you see Sharon?" Corrin said.

"No. Where is she?"

The three of us looked down at the crowded pier where hundreds of families waited behind a security fence. Corrin pulled out her cell phone and pressed the speed dial. Sharon answered.

"Where are you?" Corrin said. Sharon told her where she was standing and began waving her arm in a long sweeping arc. A lump formed in my throat.

The massive warship had stopped its forward movement. It was now inching sideways to the pier, but it didn't seem to be moving. So I ran to the starboard side, looked over the rail, and saw two tugboats, forward and aft, pushing the ship. Everything about mooring the BRIDGE was done slowly and with precision. The momentum of the 753-foot ship was too great to move any faster. Finally, the USS Bridge came to rest.

The dock crew positioned the crane and attached the gangway to the BRIDGE. What's next? I wondered. What'll I do? I wanted to follow Tim down the gangway to get a photograph of him and Sharon embracing. I also wanted a shot of Tim's expression when he saw his first-born baby. Should I allow the officers to disembark first? What was protocol?

Determined to be the first civilians off the ship, Corrin and I huddled and discussed a plan. Our luggage was already on the main deck several feet from the gangway. We were the only Tigers prepared to disembark at a moment's notice, and like true jungle tigers, we were ready to pounce.

Lieutenant Commander Andrew Weedon was the first one down the ramp. With a portable microphone in his hand, he made several brief statements and announced the names of the *first kiss* sailors, four handpicked individuals who got the honor of being the first sailors to greet their families.

Each one of them carried a single rose as they descended into the arms of their families, who met them with bouncing leaps and high-pitched screams.

Fifteen new fathers were next. One by one the executive officer announced the father's name and the calendar date of each baby's birth.

"EN3 Richards, June 21," came the call, and down the ramp he went. We stayed in place, but sprang into action when the executive officer announced liberty call at 1530 hours. Hoisting up our luggage, we stepped off the ship and onto the ramp. Corrin went first, and I was right behind her. I wanted to hang my camera around my neck to be ready for a quick picture. But I couldn't; it would swing. I needed both hands for my luggage.

The gangway had a series of wooden safety steps, one-by-four rungs set two feet apart. What if I tripped and dropped my luggage in front of the crowd?

"Don't trip!" I shouted to Corrin who swiftly high-stepped her way over the rungs and down the ramp. In the same manner, I quickly lifted and placed my feet carefully on each rung. I glanced below at Tim and Sharon. They embraced, and little Emily got gently squeezed between them.

When I arrived at the bottom, I stepped off and looked around at the excited, cheering crowd. Local newspapers and television stations were everywhere. Keyed-up sailors flowed off the ship. Children hopped around like bunny rabbits and hung on the pants of their parents. Everyone hugged and kissed and cried. It was an emotionally moving moment, but I stayed focused. I had a job to do.

Stepping next to a chain link fence to secure a place for my luggage, I quickly unzipped my camera bag and pulled out my Pentax Spotmatic II. With a quick click of the shutter, I captured the moment for life: the four of them in one shot.

Tim cradled baby Emily in his arms and looked lovingly into her round brown eyes. Then he beamed a smile bright enough to light the day. With her hands clasped in prayerful pose, Sharon proudly gazed with adoration for her husband as he held the child she had delivered while he was at sea.

And with all her love and tenderness, Aunt Corrin looked on. Her tearful eyes and curled lips expressed a great upwelling from her heart.

Tim was home from the war.

* * * * *

Captain Stockton & his wife

USS Bridge in port

EN3 Tim Richards & Emily   Sharon Richards Corrin Richards

Tim & Sharon & Emily

ADDENDUM

Journal of Corrin B. Richards
Oct 28 to Nov 5, 2003—United States Navy Tiger Cruise—USS Bridge

The ship is an amazing world in itself, full of exciting "wows" and wincing "oh"s. Although very different, Las Vegas and the USS Bridge have something in common, amazingly—no windows. Unless you go out onto the deck or look at a watch, you have no idea what time of day it is, what the weather is like, or if there is land in sight. At first, I couldn't understand why Timmy mentioned he didn't always know if it was sunny or rainy, light or dark outside. Now it makes perfect sense. If I didn't have reason to go outside on the deck for tours or events, my daily routine would take me from my berthing to the mess hall to Timmy's shop to the main space. None of those areas have a glimmer of the outside.

All ceilings inside the ship, for the most part, cannot be taller than seven feet, and there is not one wall that I have found that isn't painted steel. All doorways are cut-out ovals in the middle of steel walls, starting about a foot off the ground. This means that I carefully have to step over each lip at each door to catch myself from banging my shin or jamming my toes and tripping forward. I have found that steel is very unforgiving. Each door also has an attached door/hatch that has a steel hook and air lock mechanism to prohibit anything from passing through, should a floor or air violation occur. All hallway breaks have two of these doors. As you approach the first door, you must flip the steel hook, break the seal, and enter though. You then turn around and close that door behind you, sealing it as it was before you passed. As you proceed forward no more than four feet, there is another door of the same. Open the seal, pass through the door, and then turn around and close that door, sealing it behind you. What a process! As you move from one area in the ship to another, this is a routine you participate in at least four times… becoming quite a cumbersome task to travel from one space to another.

I am typing this to you as I sit in the "mess hall." Not dining room—mess hall. Surprisingly, the food has been pretty decent… always a square meal with a few choices. I have to remember, though, that the ship had an opportunity to "load up" on fresh fruit, dairy, and eggs when we boarded in Pearl Harbor. Timmy did not typically eat as I am eating today. When the sailors are out to sea, they go weeks at a time without grocery deliveries, making the apple I am about to eat seem like it's the greatest piece of fruit I have had in years.

We are officially underway and have seen a demo of fuel transfer to another frigate. There are two huge tubes (maybe as wide as a dinner plate and as long as a football field?) that are suspended on a wire line ... the line is shot with a gun over to the boat needing refueling, and then the men heave the line until there is no slack. After everyone is ready, they heave the fuel lines over to the other boat and connect it up. Amazing!

It is at least ninety degrees and completely free of clouds on the deck. I am roasting in my jeans and a tank top, but I am sure it is going to get much colder. The berthing (sleeping) area is freezing, though, I bet no warmer than sixty-two. From one extreme to another! The ship is identical to the submarine movies with air tight passageways that make your ears pop from one area to another as you transfer between areas.

You can definitely feel the ship moving now—it is not rocky, but you can just tell you are under motion. We draw thirty-five feet and the ship displaces 45,000 long tons.

I have never seen water this blue in my life. The ocean is royal blue, like a Crayola marker. Where the boat makes wake in the back, the water is aquamarine. Again, like a Crayola marker. I have never experienced such clear, bright colors in my life!

We had lunch: cafeteria chicken cordon blue and three-bean salad. I have been thrust back to the fourth grade cafeteria! We will be reconvening at 12:30 p.m. to have a "Tiger" meeting. We have a tour today and then some kind of Halloween party tonight where I am going to try to win back the $70 I spent to eat on the ship.

Seeing Timmy has been great. He is truly in his element! He knows every nook and cranny in the ship—from the ice cream machine parts to why the AC bearing burned out. Timmy is very modest, yet knows how to do his job ... very impressive. His superiors speak great things about him. I see the other sailors, who must have very little interaction with their superiors, and realize that Timmy is in a fantastic situation. If the fridge's generator or cooling device breaks, even the Captain doesn't eat cold food ... and Timmy knows how to fix it. If the AC blows in the middle of the Persian Gulf in 130-degree weather, the entire ship's crew, machinery, and mission is put at stake ... and Timmy knows how to fix it. They call him Jimmy Neutron on the ship—a cartoon character that is coyly smart and can pull off any feat requiring an engineering focus.

Dad is in his heyday as well. Every time Timmy tells a story about his work, Dad would reply with, "Well Tim, that just must mean you are doing an extraordinary job," and "Timmy, kids your age just don't do the amazing things you are doing!" He recites the rankings Timmy will move across, noting the rank Timmy began at and then listing the ranks he has progressed ... along with the ranks he can achieve. He knows the ins and outs of Timmy's superiors, job description, and the "extra things"

Timmy does to get ahead. He asks question upon question about Timmy's experiences, telling him to go into explicit detail when he wasn't clear about duties or how a task unrolled.

We just linked up with the USS Nimitz—what an amazingly large boat! The Nimitz is an aircraft carrier that the USS Bridge refuels on a frequent basis. They suspended a line between the two ships, and while each ship traveled at thirteen knots side by side (maybe 100 yards apart), the crew sent the Admiral across the line from one boat to another in a dangling chair. When you looked at the Nimitz from the Bridge, the two ships looked completely stagnant because they were perfectly traveling the same speed at the same time. The water here is so unbelievably blue—I wish I could swim!

I am trying to stay out of the sun, but the tours we took today and events have all been on the deck, so I am getting a lot of it! SPF 45 on my face … it is amazing how strong the sun reflects off the water! We saw H-46s, two huge cargo helicopters that are maintained on the boat. There are two sets of three propellers on the top of the helicopter, and they run on JP5, a kind of jet fuel.

I am learning my way around the ship pretty well, and I can certainly see why my poor brother has been going stir crazy. After a few days, I have no doubt I will be tired of the boat… and I just got on!

Tomorrow we have a pretty full day of tours and then a cinema night on the flight deck outside. We also have a bingo night planned in addition to karaoke. Although I can hold a mean rhythm, my tone-deaf ears will keep me from winning any karaoke contest. I will definitely not be singing on the Bridge! There is more planned, but I don't have my schedule in front of me, so I'll have to document what we're up to as time passes.

Today I shot a 50-caliber gun! I have never shot a gun in my life … but today I did! It was a machine gun-like barrel that sat as high as my shoulders, stationary on the aft port side of the ship. We waited in line to get suited up in a hard helmet, a very heavy vest (maybe lead?) and ear protection. I descended to the lower level and walked up to the gun surrounded with six Navy men dressed in cameo. The key operator/helper sailor instructed me how to use the gun by saying in less than one breath: "Step up, hold these handles here with both hands, aim out to the horizon, and just press and hold this button. Have fun!" Just like that. No hesitation. So, suddenly I was shooting sixteen shells of 50-caliber bullets into the Pacific Ocean, just like that. What a strange rush, spending two and a half seconds firing off sixteen bullets that are the length between the tip of your index finger and thumb. You feel awkwardly intrigued and somewhat excited as you feel the shells land on your shoes and the gun vibrate in your hands like a video arcade game. You also feel like you've done something terribly wrong and should runaway as fast as you can from the area.

The ship also had an extra supply of missile flares—incredibly bright white flares that light up the sky for over forty-five seconds. They are loaded into a 40-mm grenade launcher, a smaller version of a shotgun, and fired off into the sky. After my dad volunteered me to do so (why wouldn't he), I stepped up and took the gun to light up the night sky. My second gunshot of my lifetime! I shot two flares to the moon … or what felt like it, anyway.

What's a party without a star? The "class clown" of the USS Bridge, a younger gentleman with smart remarks that he shared with all from the 5:30 a.m. mess hall breakfast to the 11 p.m. karaoke sessions, suddenly appeared on the flight deck mid-picnic. Dressed in swim trunks and flip-flops and proudly strolling as if he was about to present his fellow sailors with the greatest prize of the day, he made a grand entrance, commanding the attention of all. Swung over his back was a large inflatable kiddy pool, bright with purple hippos, pink flamingos, and green palm trees—just large enough for him to awkwardly sit in. He quickly positioned himself and the pool in the middle of the deck and filled the pool with water from a hose. He certainly got laughter from all. Little did he realize that the majority of us were not laughing because he was funny… but because we all knew that the seventy-four degree windy weather combined with cold water from the hose could not possibly allow for an enjoyable "swimming" experience.

We have seen some incredibly amazing events, and that is an understatement. The air show, for one, was just breathtaking. Similar to what we have seen in Chicago, this one was complimented with no surrounding land and included an aircraft carrier, the USS Nimitz, cruising along side of us (not more than 100 yards away), serving as a starting and landing ground for the participants in the show. From helicopters to fighter jets, they were all amazing in their own unique ways.

* * * * *

APPENDIX

USS Bridge (AOE 10)
Richard V. Stockton, Captain USN

Tiger Cruise - 30 October 2003 to 05 November 2003
Pearl Harbor to Bremerton Naval Base, Washington
EN3(SW) Tim F. Richards, Corrin B. Richards, Tim J. Richards

Ship's Mission

The primary mission of the USS Bridge (AOE 10) was to conduct prompt, sustained replenishment operations at sea, providing fuel, ammunition, provisions, stores, fleet freight, mail, and personnel through a combination of alongside and vertical replacement methods in support of fleet operations. She could easily cruise for sustained periods at Battle Group speeds, replenishing and rearming the entire Battle Force.

Ship's Characteristics

o Length: 753 feet
o Beam: 107 feet
o Speed: 30+ knots
o Draft (full load): 37 feet
o Displacement: 48,500 tons
o Crew accommodations: 40 officers, 36 petty officers, and 591 enlisted

WESTPAC 2003 Deployment Facts

o Persian Gulf deployment dates: 05 MAR 03 to 05 NOV 03
o Fuel transferred: 93 million gallons
o Cargo transferred: 15,000 pallets (12,000 tons) of cargo, stores, and fleet freight transferred over to 190 U.S. and Coalition warships in support of Operations *Iraqi Freedom* and *Enduring Freedom*
o Ordnance transferred: 17,600 million pounds
o Underway replenishments: 200
o Distance traveled: 62,000 nautical miles, most over 30+ knots
o Close In Weapons Rounds Expended: 8000
o Flight hours: 836
o HC-11 SeaKnight Helicopters made over 5,500 cargo lifts, 1390 ship landings, and conducted 7 medical evacuations

o   Dental patients treated: 1,100
o   Vaccination and immunizations: 3,900

o   Reenlistments: 34
o   Reenlistment bonuses: $144,235
o   Sailors promoted: 66
o   Religious services conducted: 55

o   Navy Campus Program for Afloat College Education courses completed: 250
o   Armed Forces Vocational Aptitude Battery Tests completed: 46
o   Surface Warfare Officer Qualifications: 5
o   Enlisted Surface Warfare Specialist Qualifications: 130
o   Enlisted Air Warfare Specialist Qualifications: 3
o   Officer of the Deck Underway Qualifications: 6
o   Engineering Officer of the Watch Qualifications: 4
o   Combat Information Center Watch Officer Qualifications: 8
o   Community Relations Project Participants: 104 sailors

o   Port visits: Pearl Harbor, Maui, Hawaii; Jebel Ali and Fujairah, United Arab Emirates; the Kingdom of Bahrain; and the Republic of Singapore
o   Beer day: 28 APR
o   Swim call in the Gulf of Oman: 13 AUG

* * * * *

RESUME

EN1(SW) Timothy F. Richards
United States Navy

➢ ENLISTED in the United States Navy, 6 years, March 18, 2002, Distinguished Military Graduate in all three military schools attended (Common Core, Mechanical Core, and Engineman "A" School);

➢ ASSIGNED to USS Bridge (AOE 10), Bremerton Naval Base, Washington;

➢ Promoted to the rank of Petty Officer Third Class (E-4) in 12 months;

➢ Endured an 8-month deployment in full support of *Operations Iraqi Freedom* and *Enduring Freedom;*

➢ Awarded the *Navy and Marine Corps Achievement Medal* (NAM) for outstanding performance during the above deployment;

➢ Rapidly promoted to the rank of Petty Officer Second Class (E-5) in a period of 20 months;

➢ Earned the *Enlisted Surface Warfare Specialist* (ESWS) designation;

➢ Received 1ˢᵗ flag citation as Engineman Fireman from Rear Admiral Hering, Commander, Naval Surface Forces, PACNORWEST, as *Pacific Northwest Junior Sailor of the Quarter* (JSOQ 2Q 2003);

➢ Received 2ⁿᵈ flag citation as Engineman Third Class form Rear Admiral Hering for preparations leading to successful completion of major naval preparation exercise (Underway Demonstration, JTFX [Joint task Force Exercise], and SMA [Supply Material Assessment]);

➢ Recognized among crew of over 600 on the USS Bridge (AOE 10), including Captain, XO, and Chief Engineer, as a technical expert in his field of air conditioning and refrigeration, naval fuels, potable water production, and quality of life equipment, including galley, laundry, and habitability equipment;

➢ Personally responsible for the successful transfer over 94 million gallons of fuel and 30,000 gallons of potable water to coalition ships during *Operations Iraqi Freedom* and *Enduring Freedom*;

➢ Supervisor of two work centers, supervisor of auxiliary operations of 12 personnel;

➢ REASSIGNED as Plank Owner to newly commissioned USS Bainbridge (DG-96)

➢ May 2004; selected to participate in commissioning and arduous shake down sea trials;

➢ Received citation as Engineman Second Class from Cdr. Dorey as the first *Junior Sailor of the Quarter* USS Bainbridge;

➢ Became qualified operator of 9mm handgun, 12-gague shotgun, M14 rife, M16 rifle, and A4 close quarters rifle;

➢ Awarded *Good Conduct Medal* for 4 years of good conduct;

➢ Awarded the *Navy and Marine Crops Achievement Medal* with 1st cluster (NAM) for outstanding performance in connection with the above shake down cruise;

➢ Rapidly promoted to the rank of Petty Officer First Class (E-6) in a period of 44 months;

➢ Received 1st citation as USS Bainbridge *Sailor of the Quarter FY06 Quarter 4*;

➢ Received qualification as Engineering Duty Officer, Dec 06; overall in charge of import engineering duties in lieu of the Chief Engineer while on duty;

➢ Recognized among crew of over 300 on the USS Bainbridge (DDG-96), including Captain, XO, and Chief Engineer, as a technical expert on assigned job activities and engineering organization. First E-6 or below on this gas turbine based ship to be designated Engineering Duty Officer;

➢ Qualified as Engineering Officer of the Watch (EOOW), the highest engineering watch attainable. Directly responsible for the safe operation, maintenance, and casualty control of Engineering Department on an Arleigh Burke Guided Missile Aegis Class Destroyer during underway operations with equipment located in 3 Main Engine Rooms, and 5 Auxiliary spaces with equipment including 4 GE LM2500 25000 HP main engines, 2 mains reduction gears, 3 gas turbine generators, 5 200 ton A/C units, 3 low pressure air compressors, 2 refrigeration units, 4 steering gear high pressure pumps, and all other engineering equipment. Is directly responsible (or works in lieu of) to the Chief Engineer and reports directly to the Officer of the Deck while underway.

➢ Current status May 2007: active duty, Norfolk Naval Base, Virginia;

* * * *

MILITARY FAMILY ANCESTORS

Petty Officer First Class Timothy F. Richards descends from a long ancestral line of American military officers and enlisted men who have served in the United States Armed Forces. Presently on active duty, EN1(SW) Richards proudly stands among our family ranks of those who have volunteered in the defense of Freedom.

Summarized below are the military ancestors of our family history that span 230 years, from the Revolutionary War of 1777, the War of 1812, World War I, World War II, the Korean Conflict, the Cold War (in which the author served), and finally the War in Iraq. I am proud to say that my son, Tim is the 11th family member since World War I and the 16th since the Revolutionary War to serve our great nation.

➢ LIEUTENANT COLONEL HUGH DAVIDSON (Great grandfather 6x), Revolutionary War; commissioned March 21, 1777, Bedford County, Pennsylvania;

➢ PRIVATE ROBERT CRAIGHEAD (Great grandfather 5x), Revolutionary War; served in Captain Abraham Smith's Company, February 6, 1776, and in Captain John Alexander's Company, 7th Pennsylvania Regiment, 1778;

➢ CAPTAIN SAMUEL WALKER (Great grandfather 5x), Revolutionary War; served in General George Washington's Continental Army, Battle of Brandywine, 5th Battalion of Pennsylvania Troops. As a civilian during the War of 1812, Samuel Walker ferried General Morgan's Army across the Monongahela River in an effort to suppress the Whiskey Rebellion in western Pennsylvania;

➢ COLONEL PHILIP HOWELL (Great grandfather 4x), Revolutionary War; served 1778-1783 in Captain Thomas Morton's Troops, Militia Rangers, Westmoreland County, Pennsylvania. He was a noted Indian fighter;

➢ MAJOR JOHN WALKER (Great grandfather 4x), War of 1812. In 1803 while working as a civilian and as the owner of the Walker Boat Yards in Elizabeth, Pennsylvania, John Walker was commissioned by the President Thomas Jefferson Administration to build two pirogues (flat bottom boats) for the *Lewis and Clark Expedition, Corps of Discovery.* In 1825 he was the town's official host to the French General and Statesman Marquis de Lafayette when the Marquis toured the United States;

➢ LIEUTENANT JOHN VAN KIRK (Great uncle), World War I; served 1917-1918 in United States Navy Submarine Service. He served as the Executive Officer of the submarine K-5 that sailed up the Mississippi River at the end of the war;

➢ LIEUTENANT GEORGE T. RICHARDS, II (Great uncle), World War I; enlisted 13 August 1917; aviator, United States Expeditionary Force, Army Signal Corps, Air Service France. As a civilian during World War II, he participated in the production of the atomic bomb; Army

Service Forces, Corps of Engineers, Manhattan District; officially recognized on 6 August 1945 by Secretary of War Henry L. Stimson;

➢ MM-2 GWYNNE RICHARDS (Grandfather), World War I; USNRF, served in United States Naval Forces operating in European waters, 13 December 1918, ESB-WVC, Navy Base Hospital #2, Strathpeffer, Scotland;

➢ CAPTAIN JOHN GILMORE (1st Cousin 1R), World War II; United States Navy, 8th Amphibious Force, North Africa, Sicily, Italy, and southern France; recalled to active duty 1951 in Korean War; later served as Brigade Commander, Recruit Training Command, Bainbridge, Maryland; retired 18 October 1978;

➢ OFFICER GEORGE T. RICHARDS, III (1st Cousin 1R), World War II; 1945-1946, United States Army Corp, Piper Cub flight training, attached to B-29 squadron, Kirkland Field, Albuquerque, New Mexico;

➢ SEAMAN GWYNNE RICHARDS, JR., (Uncle), United States Navy, 1944-1946;

➢ CAPTAIN JOHN S. EDINGER (1st Cousin 1R by marriage), United States Navy, 1956, served 4 years active duty and 27 years inactive reserves; retired 1987;

➢ SPECIALIST FOURTH CLASS BARRY G. RICHARDS, (Uncle), United States Army, 1958-1960, artillery supply, Fort Bragg, North Carolina;

➢ SPECIALIST FOURTH CLASS TIMOTHY J. RICHARDS (Father), United States Army, 1961-1964, Section Chief, field artillery fire direction control (FDC), Battery A, 2nd Howitzer Battalion, 37th Artillery, 7th Corps, Dachau, Germany;

➢ PRIVATE FIRST CLASS KEVIN F. RICHARDS (1st Cousin), United States Army Reserves, 1993-1997, Clemson University, South Carolina;

➢ PETTY OFFICER FIRST CLASS TIMOTHY F. RICHARDS on active duty, United States Navy, USS Bainbridge; enlisted March 22, 2002; *Operations Iraqi Freedom* and *Enduring Freedom*, 19 March 2003 to 05 November 2003.

* * * * *